HOW TO START A YOUTUBE CHANNEL:

The Ultimate Guide For Side Hustlers

Table of Contents

Introduction 6

PART I: Why Start a YouTube Channel? 8

CHAPTER 1: New Content for a New Era......... 11

CHAPTER 2: Purpose and Programs: What's Your Niche?... 18

CHAPTER 3: Looking Ahead: Beyond YouTube 25

PART II: The Basics: How to Start a YouTube Channel 31

CHAPTER 4: Equipment: What Do You Need? 34

CHAPTER 5: Basic Tips: From Name to Art 40

CHAPTER 6: Getting Started and Maintaining Momentum 45

PART III: Beyond the Basics: How to Grow Your YouTube Channel 52

CHAPTER 7: Quality and Quantity.................. 55

CHAPTER 8: Attitude and Accountability: Avoiding Pitfalls 60

CHAPTER 9: Financial Success: Monetizing Your YouTube Channel................. 66

PART IV: YouTube Success Stories 71

Chapter 10: Arts and Entertainment 74

Chapter 11: Politics and History....................... 79

Chapter 12: Fitness and Advice........................ 84

Chapter 13: Cooking and Home....................... 90

Chapter 14: Travel and Adventure................... 95

Chapter 15: General Educational..................... 99

Conclusion... 104

Copyright 2019 by For Side Hustlers

All rights reserved.

This content is provided with the sole purpose of providing relevant information on a specific topic for which every reasonable effort has been made to ensure that it is both accurate and reasonable. Nevertheless, by purchasing this content you consent to the fact that the author, as well as the publisher, are in no way experts on the topics contained herein, regardless of any claims as such that may be made within. As such, any suggestions or recommendations that are made within are done so purely for entertainment value. It is recommended that you always consult a professional prior to undertaking any of the advice or techniques discussed within.

This is a legally binding declaration that is considered both valid and fair by both the Committee of Publishers Association and the American Bar Association and should be considered as legally binding within the United States.

The reproduction, transmission, and duplication of any of the content found herein, including any specific or extended information will be done as an illegal act regardless of the end form the information ultimately takes. This includes copied versions of the work physical, digital and audio unless express consent of the Publisher is provided beforehand. Any additional rights reserved.

Furthermore, the information that can be found within the pages described forthwith shall be considered both accurate and truthful when it comes to the recounting of facts. As such, any use, correct or incorrect, of the provided information will render the Publisher free of responsibility as to the actions taken outside of their direct purview. Regardless, there are zero scenarios where the original author or the Publisher can be deemed liable in any fashion for any damages or hardships that may result from any of the information discussed herein.

Additionally, the information in the following pages are intended only for informational purposes and should thus be thought of as universal. As befitting its nature, it is presented without assurance regarding its prolonged validity or interim quality. Trademarks that are mentioned are done without written consent and can in no way be considered an endorsement from the trademark holder.

Introduction

Starting a YouTube channel is a fun, exciting and potentially lucrative way in which to showcase your creative talents. YouTube purports to have something for everything, and you could easily be a part of that plethora of entertainment, knowledge, and advice that resides on the site. As the format for most content keeps changing rapidly, streaming is fast becoming the primary method by which most people get their entertainment and information. There are multiple opportunities for someone who has good ideas and a unique vision to jump into this arena—having fun and making money to boot.

In the course of this book, you will explore the many reasons why putting in the time and effort to create a YouTube channel is an excellent idea, from promoting a business that you already have to monetize your favorite hobby or skill. You will also learn, step by step, how to set up and run a successful YouTube channel, as well as glean some ideas of what might be possible if your channel becomes a hit—there are opportunities beyond YouTube to be gained, as well. You will also read about numerous success stories already in play on YouTube, from educational channels to cooking and home-style shows to politics and entertainment channels. There is literally content for everyone out there; you merely have to develop and promote your niche.

So, read on for both inspirational motivation and practical advice regarding how to start your own successful YouTube channel today! It only takes a bit of time, an interesting idea, and a modicum of determination to become the next YouTube sensation.

PART I:
Why Start a YouTube Channel?

Most people start a YouTube channel in order to exert some creative energy, possibly in the interest of making additional income or to turn a passionate hobby into a touchstone for others. There are also professional organizations that use YouTube as a way of reaching an audience that they would not be able to reach through traditional media outlets. Here, the purpose is to address those of you who wish to know how to start a YouTube channel, the basic nuts, and bolts, as well as how to monetize and popularize it as best you can. Thus, beyond the basic desire to share something you find funny or profound with others, there are reasons to do so using YouTube as your particular format.

First, streaming video is one of the fastest-growing formats on the internet; by most estimates, it will grow another ten percent in the next two years—now is the time to get on board with this rapidly expanding industry. Second, building a successful YouTube channel requires only basic equipment and a rudimentary understanding of production; the better you become at this, of course, the more reach your channel will likely have, but it's fairly simple and easy to get started. Third, you can reach an audience as specific or as broad as you like, depending on what you decide to broadcast and in what manner; you have more control over your content than in any traditional media outlets. It is also possible to use your YouTube channel as a tie-in to another business you have, and integrating your video content with a web site is another way to boost your viewership and reach. Finally, there are ways in which you can monetize your YouTube channel—some people have even been able to make a substantial living at it—enabling you to take it on as an actual career, or at least a significant generator of revenue. As well, if your channel is successful and unique, there are always possibilities beyond YouTube, as people have launched careers in traditional television and other entertainment venues via their YouTube experience. Basically, depending on how dedicated you are to creating your content and marketing it to others, you could have a fulfilling hobby, a bit of extra side income, or a full-on career.

Following are chapters that discuss the rise of YouTube and its continued projected growth.

YouTube has been wildly successful beyond expectation; its appeal is undeniable, from mobility and ease of use to its ability to touch on wide-ranging experiences and ideas. Next, you'll investigate how to get started with your own ideas and work on how to discover your own niche within the varied world of YouTube content. Last, the possibilities of what you might be able to do beyond YouTube once you have created and promoted a channel that becomes a sensation. The opportunities are virtually endless.

CHAPTER 1:
New Content for a New Era

The era of traditional media is fading fast, while the time of the internet and streaming content continues to grow ascendant. There are various reasons for this, of course, from the advent and ubiquity of the smartphone to the increasing speed and quality of technology coupled with the falling cost of access to it. Suffice it to say; most young and financially stable young people in the developed world are readily equipped to launch their own YouTube channel (or web site, or infamous meme, or social media sensation). This proliferation of amateur-based content is both a blessing and a curse: first, it means that many people can express many voices across the steadily growing platforms—this divergence of material gives birth to a diversity of content and an audience for almost every idea. But as the popularity of the YouTube channel venture continues to grow, this means that there is more competition in order to secure viewers and, potentially, financial gain. Thus, you must contemplate why you intend to begin your channel, what your particular purpose with the said channel is, and how you should go about creating the best content with the widest possible audience.

One of the most significant reasons to create your own YouTube channel is to recognize the far-ranging reach that this kind of content is beginning to have. If you want to reach an audience with your creative content, then you have to think beyond text these days, particularly with regard to a millennial audience. With predictions that more than three-quarters of the American population will get at least some of their video content from streaming services within the next couple of years, the time is ripe to get started on the ground floor of this ever-expanding platform. In addition, the trend with regard to social media influencers shows no signs of slowing; an entire generation of young people are shopping, buying, and exhibiting other consumer habits based on what they see on platforms like YouTube. The potential for financial growth is truly staggering. Kylie Jenner is not the world's youngest billionaire without the growth of social media video content. Also be aware that the audience size of YouTube is unprecedented, with an estimated billion and a half regular monthly users—even if you get views at a mere fraction of this, you would be doing quite well.

Promoting a business that you have already established is also an excellent reason to get behind this new platform. Whether your business is your main source of income or a side hustle to bring in some extra, a YouTube channel can greatly boost your marketing strategy. It's an excellent way to explain to customers what you do and how you do it—visual explanations have great power, of course. It also provides a large and varied customer base, as discussed above. Additionally, with a YouTube channel, you control the content itself: you can establish yourself as an expert in your field, for example, or you can show that you are a better value than your competitors; all of this strengthens consumer trust in the brand that you have created. A YouTube video is also a superb way to educate potential consumers about your products and/or services. Unlike traditional media advertising wherein a commercial is only thirty seconds long or so, your YouTube channel can provide a platform for an entire series of related commercials, themselves creatively designed and presented. It's this kind of out of the box thinking that garners small company's large followings. Not only do you gain a strong customer base, but you also gain a loyal following that will stay true to your brand. If you educate and entertain your potential customers, then you have hit the jackpot combination.

If you are a creative type, then a YouTube channel is an absolute bonus, no matter what the realm. This is a particular advantage for newcomers who are working to build an audience for their specific art. Whether it be graphic illustration, painting, sculpting, or installation work, the benefit of having a YouTube channel is that you not only reach a broad audience but you also have the means to show your creative process, thus creating an even deeper interest in your work. This can take many forms: it could be educational, with tips and techniques designed to help others take up the kind of art that you make; it could be purely visual, wherein you show exactly how you create a particular work of art (complete with matching music for mood); it could be in the style of a diarist, wherein you recount, in your series of videos, what provides you with inspiration. There is also the niche wherein you can encourage your audience to stick with it: as any creative type knows, one of the hardest parts of making art, whether visual or textual or other, is to simply sit down and stick to it. Motivational videos are another facet of the creative YouTube channel industry.

In addition, if you have a unique skill or a fascinating hobby, YouTube is a place to go to share that and inspire others. This is the place where how-to videos are in great demand. Literally, there are videos for almost every skill or hobby that is out there: from knife sharpening to furniture making to knitting to technological skills, there are how-to videos already on the platform. The way to make your channel stand out is via your own artistic designs, your personal voice, and the unique way in which you approach your videos. Conceiving of a YouTube channel as a series—not of individual videos but a closely linked set of episodic videos—is an excellent way to get a following and keep them. Think of network television or Netflix originals: these are series where each episode builds on what comes before. You are creating a narrative, not just an isolated few minutes of video. This applies to any kind of channel on YouTube, but it would certainly be a way to make the hobby genre stand out among many.

Last, all of these things could be a way in which to make money—more on that in Part III. If the YouTube channel will be your side hustle, then there are some other considerations, as well. The side hustle is a way in which those of us who wish to earn more, save more, or both can invest a little time and energy into to make a bit more cash on the side. If you already have a full-time job and a busy life, then it can be difficult to envision how you would have the time and energy left to direct to another form of employment. This is the beauty of the side hustle—very little commitment (in most cases) and enormous flexibility (in all cases). You can decide how much or how little time you invest, and especially if you are already gainfully employed, you can walk away at any time. The other unexpected advantage of a side hustle is that, in some cases, the side hustle can develop into a full-blown business opportunity in and of itself. There are countless examples of young entrepreneurs taking their side hustle into an enormously successful business. Engaging in a side hustle is a lucrative opportunity of varying degrees for anyone who wishes to increase their income or to pursue a passion while maintaining everyday stability. One of the best platforms for starting this—though it does take time and investment upfront—is the YouTube channel.

First and foremost, the side hustle shouldn't interfere with your success in your primary employment. This will be the first consideration when determining what kind of side hustle you might like to try; if it takes too much time or energy that it detracts from your stable income (remember: there is no health insurance in the side hustle), then it isn't for you. Compromising your productivity at your day job is not an advisable way in which to net any long-term gains. Crucially important to the entrepreneurial side hustle is the time factor. Be certain that you create a set schedule and stick to it. Not only do you not want to shortchange your primary employer, but you also don't want to shortchange yourself or your family. Know and acknowledge your limitations before you quickly burn out.

Starting a YouTube channel can provide numerous opportunities and, ultimately, financial benefits. If you spend enough time determining what your passion is and developing this into a coherent, cohesive set of episodes, then you are well on your way toward creating a successful site. Taking advantage of this unique medium still at the nascent stages of its reach is an undeniable win for anyone with the talent and time. In the next chapter, we will discuss what kind of niche(s) are out there for you to capitalize on in this potentially lucrative side hustle career.

CHAPTER 2:
Purpose and Programs: What's Your Niche?

The importance of a niche cannot be overstated with regard to starting a YouTube channel: without a clear idea of what kind of audience is out there waiting to respond to your unique idea *within a certain category*, you are simply spending time on a fun hobby without expecting any return on your investment of time and effort. Certainly, if you have a completely unique idea, something that defies categorization, then you should work to develop it; however, you will still need to figure out how to market that to the various audience factions that visit YouTube with regularity. There are some specific and practical ways in which to determine how your particular channel will get steady views and potentially lucrative responses.

The niche that you decide upon will essentially be the foundation of your YouTube channel: you have to tailor your material toward a kind of pre-determined audience before you begin; otherwise, you're just uploading random content with no real purpose. This is certainly not a pathway toward monetizing your channel. In addition to the overall idea of a niche, you should think about the arc of your particular set of videos, as well. Each one should have an intent—a clear purpose—in the service of a larger theme that addresses your niche audience.

First, think about what interests you most: it may be a hobby about which you are passionate; it may be a business that you desire to promote and grow; it may be a skill that is specialized that you wish to share; it may be a desire to want to entertain or delight with comedic or dramatic videos, or artistic endeavors. Typically, when starting a YouTube channel, you will already have some idea of what your niche will be because it will be something that you already like doing that you already have some skill at.

Beyond that, if you're simply interested in creating a YouTube channel just because it sounds interesting or fun to you, by all means, you certainly could. Indeed, that idea could turn out to be a niche content in and of it, documenting your journey towards creating the channel and then showing how the idea evolves. In any case, it's a good idea to start with a strong foundation, for several reasons.

First, you will have to dream up new material,

new content for a very long time (even years) before the channel achieves the level of success that you ultimately desire. Overnight sensations are rare, and even if you turn out to get that lucky, it will still be the result of having very good ideas and executing them in a competent and enjoyable way. Before you even start your channel, you should have amassed a fair bit of content to upload. Then you must be prepared to keep up should your content pick up lots of views—there is too much competition to be complacent if your channel takes off; most viewers will start looking around for something else. Thus, if you don't enjoy your main focus, then you will undoubtedly have a difficult time maintaining momentum. So, one of the most important decisions you will make is: what's my niche?

Most viewers can tell if someone is genuinely excited about what they are presenting on their channel and in their videos. If you have an authentic passion for what you are presenting, and can maintain that excitement, then you have a much better shot at making a success of the venture. We all know what it's like to be around someone who is genuinely enthusiastic about what it is that they do or enjoy; this is infectious, and we find ourselves listening, even if it isn't necessarily something that we typically do. This is the idea when creating enticing videos: be genuine, be passionate, and be persistent.

The next issue to consider is whether there is a demand for what you would like to produce. If nobody is searching for the topic or idea that you have, then nobody will be watching your videos (something to think about when naming your channel is how likely it would be to pop up in a search: more on that in Chapter 5). There are two ways to look at this conundrum: on the one hand, if you simply want to create a channel because you are fascinated by some particular hobby or interest, then you are under no pressure to worry about who will watch it. On the other hand, if you are interested in monetizing your channel—which is an assumption that I'm making regarding the readers of this book—then you will want to think about what an audience will respond to. Even if your channel is just a passion project, as it were, it doesn't hurt to think about how to name it in such a way that people will find it.

One way to find out about what people are looking for on the internet, at least in a general sense, is to use something like Google AdWords Keyword Planner. This tool allows you to set up an account (it's free in most cases) so that you can look at how many searches are being done on the keywords that relate to your project.

Basically, you can look at the average monthly searches for these keywords and determine whether competition is high, medium, or low. In some sense, having little competition may be a good thing, as your vision may truly be a unique one; however, in another sense, if nobody is searching your keywords, then nobody can find your YouTube content. It's a balancing act informed by a little bit of research, a smart sense of how appealing your content is, and a little bit of luck.

There is also Google Trends, which allows you to see what topics are trending over a certain period of time. This gives you a sense if your idea is on the upswing or downswing: if it's on the upswing, then strike while the iron is hot, as they say; if it's on the downswing, you may want to rethink your topic. The market may already be saturated, and the audience is looking for the next new thing. Also, be aware that this could be seasonal: it's simply common sense to notice that searches for "Santa" and "holiday decorations" will probably trend at certain times of the year. This goes for all sorts of hobbies and skills that depend on weather or celebrations or other time-sensitive triggers.

Another crucial component to deciding on your niche is to check out the competition. Search

YouTube channels: how many other people are putting out content that is similar to what you want to do? If that area is saturated, then it will be even harder to breakthrough, of course. By the same token, also check out the quality of the competition: even if there is a lot of content on the topic that you'd like to do, if the quality isn't very high, then you still have a chance to make an impact. The prevalence of material on the topic indicates that it's potentially worthwhile to pursue; just make sure your channel is the best and brightest of the bunch.

The other way to think about this is to conceive of your own unique vision: what can you add to this conversation that nobody else is saying? Why does the audience respond? Look at the comments and see what viewers are suggesting in both positive and negative ways; this kind of research will ultimately give you an advantage over your competition, as you can fill in the gaps and improve the way in which this topic is presented. Basically, you want to ask yourself how can you bring better value to the viewers—better production values, better creative content, better continuity, and consistency. Don't abandon a topic which you are passionate about just because somebody else out there has already taken it on; just take it on in a smart, informed way and come armed with new ideas and new perspectives for presenting the same niche material. Think about it in terms of network television success stories: just because *ER* was a hit didn't mean that *Grey's Anatomy* couldn't be one, too (the same example could be made of numerous police dramas, legal dramas, family sitcoms, and so on). They just have two very different perspectives with different presentations of the same basic material.

Finally, there are some ever-popular niches on YouTube wherein your ideas might already fit. For examples, tech videos and gaming are perennially popular, as are how-to tutorials. Food and fashion always score high rates of viewers, while weight loss and healthy living are other strong niches. Travel videos—especially if they have high production values—are quite popular. Animal videos seem never to go out of style—we can't seem to get enough of their quirky antics, but it should be noted that the best ones are in the creative control of their creator. Entertainment of all kinds is really the heart of YouTube and humorous content seems to score better than dramatic. YouTube is a place to go and have fun, explore the interesting, and revel in the unusual.

CHAPTER 3:
Looking Ahead: Beyond YouTube

Your YouTube channel is merely the start of something larger, should you choose to devote sufficient time and energy into it. This is especially true if you are conceiving of your YouTube channel as an extension of a business you already have or of a skill or talent that you'd like to develop and monetize. While it is certainly true that the vast majority of YouTubers are simply amateurs who want to have fun with the medium and share something of their lives and their interests, there are some who wish to create something more lasting, to make an impact on the culture. These are the influencers and others who eventually move beyond YouTube into a more mainstream platform. There are many ways that you can think beyond your YouTube channel, both small and great.

First, remember that a YouTube channel in our technological age really doesn't take a lot of specialized equipment and or knowledge. With a smartphone, there is very little financial investment you have to make in order to create basic videos to post on your channel. For a few hundred dollars, you can invest in some basic recording and editing equipment if you'd like to move a bit beyond the very basic. Making videos is no longer expensive or terribly time-consuming. However, if you have larger plans for your channel—such as syndication—then investing in better equipment to make more complex and greater quality videos is probably a must. The more professional your videos, the greater chance they have of breaking through to other media.

Second, think in terms of integrating your YouTube videos onto your own web site, should you have one. This is where you can make product videos or promotional advertisements that support what you already have going. This kind of cross purpose use of videos is how you want to start understanding what a YouTube channel can ultimately do for you, whether you are promoting yourself, your brand, or your products and services. This is where a YouTube channel can easily go from a hobby to a successful side hustle—or even an established career.

Third, you should also be engaging with your social media audience. Chances are that, if someone follows you on Facebook or Twitter, then they will likely follow your YouTube channel, as well. In addition, every video you post has the chance to be shared—even sometimes hitting that elusive "gone viral" status. With regard to what you can do to make your videos more visible, start thinking in terms of link building, an oft-used term in the web world that describes how to increase traffic to your content while building your reputation across sites and platforms. Posting videos to various sites helps to create more visibility across the web and increases your viewership. There is also the possibility that your videos can eventually gain you affiliations with well-known and well-respected business: for example, if you run a financial advice channel, mentioning Forbes or another established business source will give your brand a boost, as well as potentially earning a mention on their site if your content is relevant and professional enough. If your content gets a link from a trusted source, then this will build your reputation significantly. This can also get you more hits, via search engine optimization. For most of us, more visibility will simply mean syndicating your videos across sites, from YouTube to Facebook and Twitter and so on, but for those of us with financial goals in mind, the link building emphasis is undoubtedly necessary to investigate.

Last, you can also, in some cases, manage to garner direct revenue from your YouTube channel: if your channel gets enough subscribers, then you can enable ads on your videos, you can make a bit of money for every thousand or so views that you can get. This direct revenue stream probably won't be enough to support a business or career, but it can be enough to offset your production costs and help get your brand noticed and followed far beyond the channel itself.

If you are willing to follow some simple steps to getting started, then you are well on your way to a fun and entertaining pastime that could quickly turn into a financially lucrative effort. Identify who your target audience might be, and decide on your particular niche, as discussed previously. Produce a few videos before you launch your channel so that you have enough content to keep the momentum going, and then create a production schedule that you can easily follow. That kind of consistency is what fosters a loyal audience. When you start to gain a following, think about ways to optimize your channel so that it shows up in various searches and reaches more people. From there, monetizing your site is next and then potentially creating a market for your brand beyond the confines of YouTube itself.

YouTube has already launched the careers of several "YouTube stars," from entertainers to beauty brands to musical acts. Some well-known YouTubers who have been able to move beyond their starting platform are Michelle Phan, Lily Singh, and Smosh. Phan, one of the earliest YouTube "how-to" stars, posted videos on how to apply make-up that grew an extraordinarily popular following: she now has her own make-up line, Epsy, which is valued at around half a billion dollars. Singh, a rapper, actress, and vlogger, now has more than ten million subscribers and was cast in a Bollywood movie. She is reportedly the third-highest earner on YouTube. Smosh, the comedy duo, got their start all the way back with MySpace and moved to YouTube where their channel has more than 22 million subscribers. They have even produced and starred in their own film, *Smosh: The Movie*. More success stories in various genres will be discussed throughout Part IV of this book.

Not only has YouTube launched their own brand of a star, but it has also propelled the careers of other artists beyond the YouTube platform into more traditional media. There are many successful web series that have eventually made their leap into the small screen, most notably among them *Broad City* and *Drunk History* of Funny or Die. Even YouTube has created success stories like these, such as *Fred* and *The Annoying Orange*. *Fred* was launched by Lucas Cruikshank as a one-time Halloween video to share with friends, starring his character Fred Figglehorn. It was so well-received that he started a YouTube channel centered on the character with a series of episodes. This eventually was made into a Nickelodeon set of movies and a short-lived television show. *The Annoying Orange* animated series was launched by Dane Boedigheimer, wherein a talking orange harasses other fruits and vegetables with his annoying jokes. It was picked up by the Cartoon Network and turned into the television show, *The High Fructose Adventures of Annoying Orange*, which ran for two seasons. It is important to note that the success of these YouTube ventures is remarkable, given that there is no streaming giant or corporate backer to get these videos to the web; these are amateur videos who struck a chord with their ideas and their productions. While these are certainly in the minority of what you might get on YouTube—and this may not be your ultimate goal—it is worth noting that the reach of YouTube has gone far beyond its original scope. YouTube has more influence than ever today.

PART II:
The Basics: How to Start a YouTube Channel

Now that you are convinced that starting a YouTube channel is an excellent idea for one of many reasons, let's get started with the basics. The very first thing you must have—and this cannot be emphasized enough—is a passion and a drive for what it is that you wish to drive your content. Without that kind of energy, investing your time and money is likely not worth it. That's why your project begins even before you launch your channel. The more preparation and planning you put into whatever content you develop, the better equipped you are for long-term success.

The next challenge is to give yourself enough time and the right space in which to record. Creating a production schedule and sticking to it is one of the immutable keys to accomplishing your ultimate goals. Even if starting a YouTube channel may not require a lot of money upfront, it does require adequate time. If you are intent on generating success, then you must create content on a regular basis, work to promote it effectively and continue to come up with new ideas and improvements. You will need to allocate your time between writing your script (and storyboarding your ideas), shooting your videos, and editing them before upload. It depends on your work habits and talents, as well as the niche you intend to fill, to determine how much time is needed. If this is your first time to record and upload content, then this will probably be a work-in-progress, learning to utilize your time efficiently and wisely. Keep good records so that you start to learn what takes up how much time, then make an effort to streamline this once you are practiced and confident.

Finally, it is time to consider the practical process of setting up the channel itself. In the following chapter, basic equipment needs will be discussed, along with some extras in which to invest if you have the resources. It's always wise to start with the basics until you determine how much effort you'd like to expend, and how much response your content might garner. Then, naming your channel and standardizing your visuals is crucial toward creating a coherent and cohesive entity. You should also consider how to optimize your channel through the use of appropriate keywords and other techniques. Last, we'll go through some step-by-step instructions on the technological end of getting the channel up and running, along with some troubleshooting and some refining.

Whether you intend to create an entertaining channel for family, friends, and assorted others or to launch a specific brand, product, or service with an idea toward making some money (or even taking on a new career), a YouTube channel can be an avenue toward personal and professional success. It is an innovative way in which to process your ideas for a larger audience, and getting started begins with just a few simple steps.

CHAPTER 4:
Equipment: What Do You Need?

For most beginners, very basic equipment is all you need. For those who wish to grow their channel, then there is some more complex, high-tech gear that you might eventually wish to invest in. Most smartphones can give you decent—if very amateurish—videos and most laptops come armed with some basic editing equipment. Beyond that, there are some items that anyone serious enough to have done everything suggested in Part I should add to their production.

Certainly, you will need a good quality camera and microphone for any video content you wish to produce; however, what you really need depends on what kind of content you're planning to make. For example, if you are doing how-to videos using Photoshop or some such program, then you don't necessarily need to invest in an excellent video camera. Still, to keep your options flexible, that's undoubtedly a good idea. The primary concern is that you shoot in HD, but when you're just starting out a basic camera should do. A helpful list of particular brands that many YouTubers use for all sorts of equipment can be found at <u>Vlogger Gear</u>.

A quality microphone is also a must-have for any decent video—in fact, in some ways, it's more important than camera quality. A video with poor audio, no matter how clever or well-conceived, will have your audience quickly tuning out. If they can't understand what's being said, then any entertainment or instructional value is lost. Again, it's not crucial that you invest in a top-line microphone right at first, but be sure to get a decent one in order for your venture not to fizzle before it even gets started. See the previous link for some suggestions here, as well.

A tripod is another piece of equipment that you'll need to make good—that is, not shaky—videos. As a very basic piece of equipment, it's a fairly easy decision to make. Pretty much any kind of tripod will do for most needs.

Lighting equipment, while not absolutely necessary for the beginner or the strict hobbyist creator, can make all the difference in the world between producing a fun, amateurish video and a slick, professional-looking one. Before you invest in any lighting equipment, however, think about where you will be filming: primarily indoors or outdoors? This is also important when thinking about other equipment, as well: will you be shooting in noisy public places, or in the privacy of your own room? Knowing these factors will greatly enhance your ability to choose the best and the right equipment for your needs.

Certainly, you will also need some sort of editing software, whether it is free (such as Windows Movie Maker) or otherwise. If you are a beginner, it's best to just use free, basic editing software before you spend a lot of money. Some other good products you can try for free are as follows: OpenShot for Windows, Mac, and Linux is a multipurpose and multifaceted editing software; it's an excellent open-source option to try out before you consider investing in expensive software, as it does much of what any paid program will do. It is also VideoPad for Windows and Mac with very basic features, and Freemake Video Converter for Windows, which allows you both to edit your videos and convert them to other formats within one program. VSDC Free Video Editor for Windows has a lot of features like OpenShot, though some have noted that it's not as user-friendly. iMovie for Mac and Movie Maker for Windows (as mentioned above) are the two basic editing software packages that come with the two operating systems, respectively. Any of these free sources should get you well on your way to producing good quality videos for your channel.

Serious YouTubers often invest in more specialized equipment, as well. This may not be the thing to do when you are just beginning, but if you have the drive and the financial resources, these are some other items you might consider. The <u>Adorama Learning Center</u> recommends some particular brands if you'd like to check them out.

Lenses can really improve the quality of your images. The size of your lens (from 18mm to 200mm) depends on what kind of shooting you will be doing, with the cost increasing as size increases. You might also think of prime lenses and zoom lenses. Prime lenses are sharper and generally cheaper than zooms, though again, what you require will depend on what and how you are shooting.

Filters are another piece of specialized equipment that will expand the realm of your creativity in the shooting. Filters can also help you shoot in settings that are not quite ideal (such as low light or very bright light, for examples). They can also help you set the mood for your video with their ability to either enhance or dampen brightness and color.

An even more specialized piece of equipment is a slider, which allows you to both stabilize and control the movement of your camera. Sliders allow you to make panoramic shots without the shakiness of handheld, of course, and a gimbal is an excellent tool for tracking shots. These pieces can take a video series and make it look like a professional shot series for a streaming service or mainstream television. This investment is best done after you've already been working with all the basic equipment for some time.

There are other professional level pieces that the most dedicated YouTuber might consider, such as grip and gaff gear, external monitor/recorder, and follow focus. Again, start with a decent camera and a solid microphone, along with some free editing software, and you're well on your way to creating a fun, entertaining, or educational YouTube channel—worry about the more expensive stuff once you reach that learning curve.

Finally, the best equipment you can have, in the end, is curiosity and commitment, a desire to produce good content and to keep learning and improving. YouTube isn't only the place for you to start your own channel, but it is also an educational resource in its own right: spend some time reviewing some popular channels, of course, and also look to some instructional videos from other YouTubers about how they make their own videos. There is a plethora of advice available for anyone to capitalize on their passion or hobby. And remember: even some of the biggest budgeted Hollywood movies turn out terribly. Why? Because they lack a good story with good characterization and good writing. All of the expensive equipment in the world will not make up for lapses in the basic arena of storytelling.

CHAPTER 5:
Basic Tips: From Name to Art

Now that you have ruminated over what your niche will be and come up with some fabulous content—ideas, scripts, production schedule, some edited episodes—you need to think about what you will call your channel and how you will present it to your potential YouTube viewers. While it may not immediately seem like the most important thing, the name you choose for your channel is the first impression a viewer will have of your content—and the thing that will draw people into your channel via their searches. You also need to consider not only how your videos themselves will look, as discussed previously, but also how the art for your channel itself will be displayed. There are some basic guidelines for both, choosing a great name and displaying your channel in a pleasing way.

The name that you choose for your channel will represent you, first and foremost, and should indicate what you consider to be your core message. There is a balance to consider between choosing a name that is too broad and one that is too narrow: too broad and your targeted audience may not know exactly what to expect from your channel, and you risk not getting much initial interest; too narrow and you risk not being able to expand your channel at some point in the future. Keep it relevant to your main interest, of course, but do think about allowing yourself some flexibility to broaden your content or shift your scope.

It's also best to keep your name concise. The more complicated and lengthy the name, the harder it is to remember. Something short and punchy is the best way to draw people in. It's the first impression they have, so make sure it's fun and representative of what you're doing with your channel. As they used to say about Hollywood, the best names were short, powerful, and easy to put into lights—now, instead of a movie marquee, it's a YouTube banner that you're thinking about.

Usually, you should avoid using hard to pronounce or esoteric words within your name. Just as with names that are too long, names that are unpronounceable or too obscure won't stick in people's minds for very long.

One of the biggest pitfalls to avoid when setting up your username is employing numbers. Say the username you want is already taken, so you just add a couple of numbers at the end, like your birthday—it's a common practice when setting up email accounts and other kinds of online content. But with YouTube, this is both confusing—who's to say which name is whose, in the end—and perceived as unprofessional. If the username you want is taken, think of another one rather than tacking on numbers.

Wordplay is always an excellent way to get people to remember your channel, as well as to be intrigued by it before they even get to the videos themselves. This could include rhyming, like "Ready Spaghetti" for an Italian cooking channel, for example, or using alliteration, like "Words for Writers" for an informative channel on writing technique. Puns and other kinds of wordplay are also fun and memorable. Check out Veritasium, which is a play on the Latin word for truth with the Greek ending for learning academies (our word gymnasium is derived from the Greek, for example).

If, for some reason, you run out of ideas or your username happens to be taken, there are username generators out there on the web that can help you. Spinxo, for example, will assist you by throwing out some potential usernames based on keywords that you give it.

If you'd rather do the brainstorming yourself,

there are a few basic ways that you can get started with the process. First, write down some words that describe you, especially in relation to what it is that you are trying to do with your videos. Why did you pick this topic? What does it say about you? How would you describe yourself in general? A list of words to start with might help you formulate a final name. Another way to get the creative juices flowing is to think of synonyms for the words that you think describe you and/or your channel. So, instead of advice, if you're doing a how-to channel, try counsel (if your name starts with a hard "C" sound, all the better: Catherine's Counsel, for example). Once you have a decent list of interesting words, start mixing them up, putting them together in various ways: eventually, you'll hit upon a snappy, powerful, and unique name for your channel.

You also need to come up with a unique and interesting presentation for your channel itself. There are two kinds of artwork that are important to the look of your channel: channel art, which is your header or banner, and channel icon, which is like your logo. Depending on your subject matter, the look of your channel art and icon can vary widely, but for the most part, you're aiming for something welcoming and interesting—something that people may not have seen before, at least in this way, that invites them to want to subscribe. Aside from that, there are some basic guidelines that you must take into consideration when designing your channel's look: first, the header must be 2560 x 1440 px so that it displays correctly across devices (even on television). Second, any text you include must be placed in the middle so it will display consistently across devices. You can design your art yourself, of course, if you follow the above guidelines alongside some more detailed advice for an even better result. Some instructions and advice are available at [G2 Learning Hub](#).

If you don't feel expert enough to design good channel art and channel icon, then you can always use a template. The templates won't be entirely unique, of course, but they offer you the opportunity to get started quickly and easily. You just put your own text within the design template provided. You can find these at [Visme](#), for one. Or, you could hire a professional if you are dedicated to the look and feel of your site. There are places online where you can hire a graphic designer for relatively cheap, such as Fiverr.

These are just a couple of the considerations that you need to take in when setting up your original YouTube channel. With a good concept, some basic equipment, a solid production plan, and a nice-looking channel with a catchy name, it's only a matter of time before you are racking up the views!

CHAPTER 6:
Getting Started and Maintaining Momentum

Now that you have gotten the entire behind-the-scenes basics ready to go, it's time to actually set up the channel itself and get going with your success. After getting everything up and running, it's a matter of maintaining momentum to increase your viewership and improve your ideas, as well as expand your reach.

First, you need to have a Google account: Google owns YouTube so the only way you can get set up is if you have a Google account. After you have that account, open up YouTube. There will be an icon in the top right-hand corner that will be your user account icon; it should be a dark green circle with the first initial of your username within it. Click that icon and find My Channel. When you click on that, it will automatically use the username you set up for your Google account; if you wish to use something different, click on the option that says "Use a business or other name." The type that in and then click "Create Channel."

Now you need to customize your channel. First, you will add your channel art, as discussed in the previous chapter, click on the button in the center of the banner. YouTube will show you how your channel art will look across devices, from computer screens to television screens to mobile devices. Make sure that it is readable and well placed in each scenario. To upload your channel icon, go to the left-hand side of the display where you will see a red box with a faceless image in it. Click and add your icon there; this is what everyone will see next to each of your uploads and across content platforms.

One of the most important parts of setting up your YouTube channel is in your description. Once you've added your channel art and icon, click on the About button to the right of the top of the page. Here is where you will enter the complete description of what your channel is about. You have up to 1000 characters in which to do this, so be sure to make the best use of the available space. It should be catchy, coherent, and enthusiastic. When a potential viewer comes to your channel, he or she will want to know what this content is all about. It will either keep them there or send them elsewhere, so spend some quality time coming up with your description. Another crucially important element within your description is to add keywords that will enable your channel to pop up when viewers are searching for YouTube.

There is also a way to add links to your channel so that viewers can also connect to your web site (should you have one) or your social media pages. It's located to the bottom right of the banner itself. This is a good way to get integration among your various sites, broadening your viewer/reader/customer base.

Once your design is in place, then you want to make sure to verify your channel. This allows you access to perks like thumbnails, adding sponsorships, and the ability to upload longer content. Find YouTube features while you are logged into your account, and click the "verify" button. Follow the instructions there (a verification code will be sent via phone or text) to ensure that your account is fully verified. Now you are ready to start uploading videos right away.

For a more visually oriented guide to how to set up the account, you can check out the step-by-step instruction at [DrSoft]().

Now that your channel is up and running, there are a few tips and techniques for those of you who are new to YouTube, ways in which you can get more views and keep your momentum moving forward. First, it is a good idea to create a trailer for your channel—this is a way for people who have not already subscribed to your channel to take a sneak peek, as it were, to find out what you're all about. We're all used to trailers at the movie theater, teasers to get us interested in the next coming attraction. Think about your trailer in much the same: give viewers a taste of what you have to offer, and make it enticing enough that they want to subscribe right away. Your trailer should be visually compelling, of course, and you should add annotations asking people to subscribe.

When uploading your videos, also think about catchy titles and smart visuals. The thumbnail image and video title are what any viewer will see before they actually watch the video itself. Keep these fresh and consistent, and customize them to your individual content for the best results.

Consistency is also key across the board for maintaining a successful YouTube channel. This doesn't merely mean that the content across the channel remain somehow cohesive and relevant to how the channel represents itself; it also applies to when you are adding content. If you have a viewership that is used to seeing one new video a week, but then you get too busy or go out of town and don't upload a video for a month, you will undoubtedly lose some traction. Set yourself a realistic schedule, and decide how often you plan to add new content. Once a month is fine if that's the expectation you set; just be sure that your audience's expectation is met by your production schedule. This is one reason why it's a good idea to have a few videos already on hand before even starting your channel. Remember: content is changing and growing ever more rapidly, and viewers move on from one thing to the next with rapidity. One of the great predictors of success is how diligent you are in keeping with the goals and expectations you set.

Make sure you also focus on optimization within the YouTube search. You want as many people to find your channel as possible, using popular and comprehensible keywords. There are videos and other sources for advice on how to optimize your search parameters, many on YouTube itself. You also want to familiarize yourself with YouTube's video ranking system, so that you know how to navigate the system, ultimately getting the best exposure for your channel.

You might want to organize your videos into playlists, once you have uploaded a sturdy amount. This is quite simply one of the best audience retention tools you have: if a viewer watches one video in a playlist, it is likely that he or she will watch the other nine, as well. Audience retention is a factor in YouTube rankings, so making playlists is a way to keep your rankings up. Be sure to add videos to playlists as you go, expanding along the way.

One of the best pieces of advice you can take heed of is to watch a bunch of other YouTube videos—and don't just stick with what's in your niche, reach out and see what else is going on in other areas. This is one of the best ways to see what other creative, educational, and entertaining people are out there doing. It will give your ideas and inspiration, as well as show you how to get better at doing some basic things. The more familiar you are with how the entire platform functions—especially with what works well—the more your own channel will benefit from that knowledge.

In addition, don't simply watch other videos, become a part of the community. The entire online experience is based on interconnectivity, of course, and you should both share your content and connect with others to see how you fit into that larger platform. This includes sharing on social media and seeking out forums wherein others are discussing issues within your niche. Posting your videos in places like Reddit and Quora can help you connect with a network of people focusing on the same kinds of content that you are. Helping to solve problems for others also naturally helps you to begin to solve problems of your own; you can learn much from the kind of networking that these platforms allow.

Finally, focus on the constant goal of continual improvement. Each time you post a video, think of something—however minor—that you could improve upon it and implement that improvement into your next video. As with any technical skill, learning to use YouTube to the best your ability takes time; there is a learning curve that will pick up speed and momentum the more often you spend looking at videos and perfecting your own. Don't lose sight of why got you into this process in the first place—stay inspired by your original material, and gets inspiration from others doing creative innovations. Look to Part IV and some of the success stories that will be related there to help you stay focused and motivated on building the best channel possible. Lastly, don't be discouraged if it takes a while to amass viewers and find your following. These things take time, some skill, and a little bit of luck to get going; be patient, and keep your eye on the prize!

PART III:
Beyond the Basics: How to Grow Your YouTube Channel

Many of the most basic tips and techniques have already been addressed with how to maintain your momentum with your channel, but there are some other suggestions for how to keep it growing, improving, and attracting new viewers. Some very simple ways in which to do this is to focus on quality: the more that you are able to grow your skills set and make the highest quality video you can, the faster your channel will garner views and praise. Investing in better equipment at that point might be one way to do it, but simple practice and some time spent reviewing others' work can also improve the quality of what you are uploading.

In addition, you can also think about growing the number of your videos. One of the keys to long-term success on YouTube is to post regularly and consistently. A lack of schedule or an overlong absence can impact the number of viewers you get in a significant way. You shouldn't sacrifice quality for quantity, of course, but these two go hand-in-hand for the most successful YouTube channels.

There is also maintaining a positive attitude. As with everything that we share on social media, there will inevitably critics and naysayers—and sometimes these responses can be quite negative. Your ability to rise above the fray and be proud of what you're doing no matter what the comments may be, and to keep your commitment to the project will all help you to stay focused on the long goal here. It's not just attitude with regard to reacting to criticism, of course; it is also key to avoid the pitfalls that come from having an overly cavalier attitude toward what you are posting, as well. One of the major pitfalls in the current social atmosphere is that of insensitively offending. Now, this is not to suggest that the "thought police" or "political correctness czars" are monitoring your every idea and presentation, but it is to be aware of how what you think and say can be taken out of context if you aren't careful. It's also simple decency to take into consideration the perspectives of others, and it is one of the foundational aspects of living together within a democratic society. YouTube has tried to negotiate these spaces, especially of late, but it is always something to take into consideration.

Your digital footprint is, in some ways, your legacy, and it can linger for many, many years. You want to cultivate an image that you are proud to own rather than quick to disown.

Finally, many people start a YouTube channel with the idea that this can be an excellent way to make some extra money—and even more than that, as some YouTube stars have shown us in recent years. We will look at ways to monetize your channel and utilize your ideas and hard work toward some kind of financial gain. Creating a YouTube channel is one of the most enjoyable side hustles out there, once you just get started.

CHAPTER 7:
Quality and Quantity

We have already talked about both quality and quantity with regard to making videos and building a reputation on YouTube. Here, we will focus on some of the specific steps that can help you make the best videos and, ideally, get the most views for your channel. There are numerous ways that can boost your viewership beyond the technical ones of optimizing and networking.

In terms of quality videos, there are the obvious routes of improving your equipment, as discussed in Chapter 4, as well as practicing your technique, even taking a class online or otherwise. Quality videos are important for a larger viewership, as is consistency. Another way to broaden your viewership is to increase your relevancy. For one, keep abreast of what is going on in current events: videos that reflect the news of the day, whether it be political or entertainment or other, often attract an audience who are interested in what ordinary people have to say about the day's events. You can also use this tip by responding to other popular channels on YouTube, though be wary of appearing negative or cynical—those other videos are popular for a reason. Another surefire way to attract viewers—this time-tested technique has led to countless memes and viral videos over the last decade or so—is to up the ante on the "cute" factor. This could include anything from adorable animals to babbling babies to emotional events; it's almost certain that you've seen a handful of these before. The trick to any of these tips, however, is to stay within the confines of your larger idea; that is, don't randomly include a "cute" video or a commentary on a hardcore news event if it doesn't already go with your fundamental vision. If your channel becomes muddled or confusing—if viewers don't know what they'll get—then you'll squander what audience you already had, rather than growing it. But if a current event or acute happenstance seems to fit in with your core message, by all means, try these out.

With regard to the technical aspects of improving quality, there are a couple of other ideas that could boost the quality of what you're filming. For example, think about investing in a green screen, which will allow you to be creative when imposing your backgrounds. In fact, a green screen can make even the most fantastical ideas come realistically true within the confines of your video. Think about backgrounds, in general, when filming. The inside of your bedroom becomes rather flat after a number of videos; venture out, and see what else might strike you fancy and be visually appealing to a broader audience.

Another way to increase the number of views per video is to learn how to embed tags in a useful way. If you are only using the most popular tags, then your video is only one out of many in any search, perhaps buried beneath more established channels. Unique—but accurate—tags help your videos stand out in the crowd. The way in which YouTube sorts videos is first by title, then by description, then by tag, so all three of these should contain important keywords that will be flagged in a search. You should also put tags within your description, ideally a number of them that will narrow the search results in one sense, but snag a larger number of viewers in another sense. These are all considerations in growing your audience over time.

With regard to quantity, this is a difficult balance to strike: how much is too little; how many are too many? You should also never sacrifice quality for quantity. However, as noted previously, viewers do expect you to post regularly, especially once you have an established viewership. Variations in your scheduled postings can affect how many views your videos get. Still, your focus should clearly remain on filming and posting videos that cohere to your overall idea and meet the utmost standards of quality that you are capable of producing.

Basically, the pathway toward creating a successful channel and gaining momentum is to focus on these following things in the following order: generating ideas, writing scripts, maintaining a production schedule, and readying some edited episodes. Often, ideas are the most important part of the process—even if you are a polished filmmaker, your channel will fall flat if the ideas aren't unique and interesting. The opposite can also be true: even if you are an amateur videographer, if you have strong ideas and good scripts, your channel might become a success anyway—and all the better, because then you can focus on improving video quality knowing that your story is strong. Along these lines, it is also important to note that the difference between good YouTube channels and mediocre ones is in the scripting: many beginners make the mistake of thinking that their ideas are good enough that they can just speak extemporaneously, without a clear scripted focus or any kind of rehearsal. While there is a certain contingent of videos that are well-suited to that kind of rawness and unscripted improvising, they are limited to performers who are truly talented and (behind the scenes) truly practiced.

Additionally, creating a production schedule is a crucial part of the process if you intend to keep up with the pace of filming. You need time to generate ideas for new episodes, along with time for writing script and rehearsing before the final filming. For a brief episode, this might take a week of planning. A day or two of brainstorming followed by a day or two of scripting, then a day of rehearsal before final shooting. Depending on how your time is allotted with regard to other professional work, this can easily be condensed into a weekend—albeit a hard-working weekend. Finally, you must allow some time for the editing process before you're ready to post the final version. Once you have a handful of ready episodes to post, start your channel, and work on the aforementioned ways to grow your audience. But don't forget to continue to brainstorm, script, rehearse, and film new episodes—because when your channel gets hot, you must be prepared to take full advantage!

CHAPTER 8:
Attitude and Accountability: Avoiding Pitfalls

Avoiding pitfalls is really a twofold issue: on the one hand, maintaining a positive attitude about your online presence and the comments it might generate is sometimes difficult; on the other hand, we must be accountable for how we represent ourselves on social media and other online platforms. Additionally, with regard to the practical nature of running a YouTube channel, there are pitfalls to avoid about how you keep your channel going and growing, many of which we've addressed before.

First, attitude is everything, as they say, and it can often be hard to stay positive when those around you go negative. Still, as Michelle Obama famously said, "When they go low, we go high." This is an excellent attitude to adopt whenever your channel gets a negative review. While one never enjoys a less than positive review, it is nigh impossible to avoid—it's pretty much an inevitable response in the vagaries of the online universe. It is also the case, however disheartening, that most negative comments aren't constructive criticism—that is, they don't provide a helpful critique as to how you might improve—but rather snide or downright ugly comments that exist only to provide some inappropriate sense of superiority to the person posting. This is a fact of life regarding the internet in general, and if you are putting your best work out there for people to judge, this can be extraordinarily difficult to brush off. Still, it is really the only appropriate response you can have, simply to acknowledge that the negative comments may or may not have anything to do with you and—most crucially—to avoid engaging in sort of back and forth. This will accomplish nothing but to make you appear thin-skinned and unprofessional.

In addition to staying positive among the negative, you must also be careful to understand and acknowledge that you are, ultimately, accountable for what you post. Even if your material is the most upbeat and innocuous, you can still garner negative comments, but if your material is deliberately provocative and/or downright offensive, then you should be prepared for a mass of feedback. In an era where there is increasing attention brought to attitudes that are considered sexist, racist, homophobic or otherwise dismissive of various groups of people, it is difficult to overstate the importance of keeping your behavior within the confines of respectfulness and thoughtfulness. Again, this isn't about policing thought or hampering thought-out opinion, but it is to suggest that you carefully consider your views if others find them offensive.

YouTube policy guidelines clearly state what will get your channel terminated: repeated violations of their Community Guidelines, any kind of predatory behavior, the use of spam, or any channel devoted to hate speech, harassment, or false impersonation (different from parody). The Community Guidelines cover all of this in greater detail. Nudity or explicit sexual content is verboten on the platform; this is not a space for pornography or graphic sexual detail. As well, if any of this involves children, YouTube will report to the authorities. Content that encourages dangerous or harmful behavior is also banned, as is overly violent and graphic content—with the caveat that if it is carefully explained in the context of newsworthy events, it might be allowed. Proceed with caution, however. Harassment, cyberbullying, and any threatening behavior—such as intimidation or invasion of others' privacy—are also policed carefully and will result in the termination of your channel. Hateful content is also barred from the sight, and deliberately invoking hatred based on race, religion, gender, sexual orientation, age, nationality, disability, or veteran status is explicitly prohibited. Now, many argue that YouTube has not done enough to police this kind of hateful content, but there have been upticks in the patrolling and removing of those sites as of late. YouTube also prohibits the use of spam (misleading descriptions and/or tags, large amounts of unwanted, unwarranted, repetitive content), and it expressly forbids the breaking of copyright laws—though that is another area wherein many argue YouTube must improve. If you have any doubt whether your channel or any of your videos may violate one of these policies, it would be a good idea to review what YouTube itself has to say at their <u>Community Guidelines</u> page. Sometimes it's a very good idea to have a friend or colleague review your work, as well; a different set of eyes can sometimes see more clearly than your own. We can all get a little too attached to our work at times and fail to see that we might have crossed a line, if not into clear policy violation, then into poor taste and sloppy thought.

Finally, with regard to the technical pitfalls that you can avoid on your YouTube channel, these are variations on what we've discussed in previous chapters about growing your channel and keeping viewers. First, be sure to optimize your videos, creating effective descriptions and specific tags so that they show up in searches. Second, make sure to create custom thumbnails to advertise the excellence of your videos—this first impression hooks viewers and, hopefully, your work keeps them staying; this is why playlists are also important. Use social media, as well, to utilize the connections you already have and bring them into your YouTube space in addition to your other online ventures. Capitalize on an audience you already know you have—this is especially important if you decide to monetize your channel. There is also something to be gained from communicating with your viewers. While you probably want to avoid responding to senselessly negative comments, it is almost always a good idea to respond to positive or helpful comments: this fosters a relationship between you and your viewers that make them feel a part of your content in a more personal way. In addition, it keeps people talking about your videos, which is nearly always a positive thing. Last, if you are creating your channel to promote your business or your brand, beware of being too pushy; we have all been annoyed by the salesperson who won't take no for an answer, or just plain won't leave us alone while we shop. If your channel sounds too much like a series of commercials, then it probably won't be as successful. This is when creating an effective and coherent storyline can assist—the marketing is hidden therein.

CHAPTER 9:
Financial Success: Monetizing Your YouTube Channel

Even if you didn't originally intend for your YouTube channel to be a way in which to bring in revenue, you might find that, if it becomes popular enough and you're enjoying the experience, then it stands to reason that you should begin to earn money from the process. This could be anywhere from enough income to invest in better quality production equipment to becoming a highly paid influencer. There are some rules and regulations that you must follow when deciding to monetize your channel, as well as some suggestions as to what are the most successful ways of capitalizing on your channel once you reach the basic requirements.

First, in order to be eligible for monetizing your YouTube channel, you must enroll in the YouTube Partner Program (YPP). This requires a few things, the most important of which is that your channel must have more than 4000 hours of views on your videos within the previous twelve months of applying, and you must have more than 1000 subscribers. This is in addition to following YPP policies and procedures. You also have to have a linked AdSense account (and only one account), which is how you will get paid. (This is easily set up online.) The instructions for how to apply for YPP is on the [YouTube Help](#) page. If your application is successful, you now have access to Creator Support teams, Copyright Match tools, and the features that will allow you to monetize your channel.

The ways to make money via YouTube are numerous. Once you are accepted into the YPP, you can make money off of advertising; YouTube will inevitably place ads on your videos, so you might as well capitalize on that once you reach viewership guidelines. You can also offer channel memberships, wherein you subscribers pay a monthly amount for special perks and benefits from you and your content. If you have an official brand, you are allowed to sell that branded merchandise showcased on your watch pages. There is also the Super Chat, where your fans can pay to have their comments highlighted. Finally, there is YouTube Premium Review wherein you get a small part of what premium users pay for their YouTube subscriptions when they view your videos. Each one of these has specific guidelines and thresholds to meet; you can review those on <u>YouTube Help</u>, as well.

There are other ways to monetize your YouTube channel, as well. If you already have an existing business selling a particular product, YouTube is a great way to garner more customers. Provide video content that showcases your product (though remember to avoid direct advertising, as mentioned in the previous chapter), then provide your viewer with an opt-in so that you can send them emails. By doing this, you create a direct relationship with the viewer, and he or she with your product. It's an excellent way in which to increase sales.

Affiliate marketing is another revenue avenue for YouTube. This is where you can do product reviews ("unboxing" videos have become increasingly popular) and provide the affiliate link. You get paid for promoting products that your subscribers buy—this is the start of the internet influencer. This kind of monetizing can be hazardous if you're not careful. Be sure to follow any and all company guidelines, YouTube regulations, and you should *always* disclose that you are, in fact, a paid associate of the company whose products you are endorsing.

You can also garner brand sponsorship for your YouTube page. This first became popular among highly regarded bloggers and has now spread to YouTube. Pitch your ideas to companies that you think might be interested in what you're doing with your channel, and see if you can get sponsorships. This monetizing tool also comes fraught with similar pitfalls as affiliate marketing: be sure to follow Google's paid product placement guidelines, as well as to disclose that you are, in fact, a paid promoter.

There is also the Amazon Influencer account, introduced a couple of years ago. This is where influencers on Facebook, Twitter, YouTube, and other social media sources can make additional money by creating Amazon ad pages filled with products they love. Every time someone buys a product from your page, you receive a commission. This isn't available to everyone, however, as you need to be an actual influencer of some sort. Once your YouTube channel is popular enough, you have a good shot at being able to engage in this kind of monetization.

Essentially, you must focus on building your YouTube channel before you can even begin to think about monetizing it. The two most crucial elements to get that audience are to create excellent content and utilize SEO (search engine optimization) to its greatest effect—using effective keywords your video descriptions and tags. The more often your videos pop up in a search, the more views you get and the more subscribers you amass. Be sure to encourage viewers to subscribe to your channel with each and every video you upload—remember that you must have more than 1000 to even think about monetizing your channel. Another thing to remember is to encourage your subscribers to share your videos on social media platforms, using networking to draw on a larger and larger audience. Subscribers are also notified each time you upload a new video, so the chances that each individual video is viewed rises with the number of subscribers you get. The best plan to eventually make money from YouTube is to start out with a clear strategy (both in your ideas and in your promotions), do adequate research on what's trending on YouTube and how to use SEO to your best advantage, and connect everything that you produce online for the greatest results.

PART IV:
YouTube Success Stories

There are countless success stories emanating from various corners of the web, perhaps none more so than from YouTube. Not only are there any number of mainstream stars that got their start on YouTube—Justin Bieber, Ed Sheeran, Bo Burnham, to name a few—but there are now numerous YouTube stars in their own right. Becoming a success on YouTube is its own pathway to financial and professional success, with more avenues than ever to achieve that, from beauty influencer to gamer to comedy act. Whatever the case may be, YouTube continues to grow and expand in its ability to foster enormous success in the many young and tech-savvy groups to which it caters.

Success can be defined in many ways, of course: there are people who have used the internet, and YouTube in particular, to start or expand a business; there are those who have used it to showcase their artistic talents, with music being one of the most well-suited to the medium; there are those who simply post their quirky points of view on YouTube, attracting viewers looking for a fun distraction in the middle of a workday or in the evening before bed. That's one of the most attractive elements about YouTube: both authorship and viewership are diverse, wide-ranging, and therefore the platform is open to nearly anyone with a little bit of time and a creatively developed idea.

Now that YouTube popularity has skyrocketed in the past few years, it may seem a more than daunting progress to try to jump in at this point; however, there are no signs to indicate that YouTube's rapid growth is slowing any time soon. In fact, now might be the best time to jump on board, as the platform has rolled out new incentives and new guidelines in the past couple of years; there are more opportunities to monetize your channel, and as with many successful organizations, success often begets even more success. Music and television producers, in particular, have begun assigning people and groups to comb through the platform regularly, looking for raw talent to develop. This is also increasingly happening in the corporate world, as sponsorships and affiliate marketing have taken off on the platform, as well. That is to say, as visible as YouTube has been for quite a while, it is becoming even more visible to traditional media powers—the time couldn't be riper to put your efforts, talents, and time into creating something that might catch the eye of a well-known producer. Short of that, it's still a good time to put your content out there, even if it stays a simple side hustle. The examples in the following chapters will both address success stories that have been newsworthy in recent years, as well as note particular channels that are both popular and representative of success within their niches. Use this information to inspire you to put out the best channel you can possibly create.

Chapter 10:
Arts and Entertainment

Of course, one of the most popular offerings on YouTube is within the realm of arts and entertainment, and the music industry seems to have benefitted the most from this new outsourcing of young talent. Comedians of various stripes have also done well, and YouTube and other online platforms have catapulted many small web-based shows to more mainstream stardom. In addition, there are YouTube stars in their own right—those who rake in large earnings and garner a vast following without a major label or production company backing. Following are some stories of successful YouTube artists and channels that are still enjoying huge followings and enormous popularity.

Just about anyone who has followed pop music over the last decade or so will know that Justin Bieber, a wildly successful young musician with a more than devoted following, got his start of YouTube. There is also the recent ascendency of Shawn Mendes, another precocious poster of charming videos with thoughtful music. And who can forget the meteoric rise of Ed Sheeran, the slightly goofy guy next door with the lovely voice and the touching melodies? All three of these young men originally spent time recording themselves singing and talking about their music, only to be signed by major music labels and launching onward to international fame and success. Lest we leave out the ladies, Alessia Cara and Carly Rae Jepsen also got their initial boost via YouTube (Jensen with the help of none other than Bieber himself). Even well-established musical artists, such as Taylor Swift and Ariana Grande, have turned to YouTube to promote their work and broaden their audience.

Other kinds of musical acts have also taken YouTube by storm. There is the highly popular group, Pentatonix, who create original mash-ups of popular songs, thereby creating something new—and doing this all with mere vocal talent, rather than relying on instruments and slick production techniques. The success of the movie *Pitch Perfect* and its subsequent sequels are certainly a contributing factor to the achievements of Pentatonix, but with two Grammy awards under their belts, there is no denying that they have a talent and reach of their own. Another kind of musical channel, Spinnin' Records showcases the talents and passions of DJs, focusing on dance music, and is ranked one of the most popular channels currently operating on YouTube.

Comedy has also been an excellent draw for the audiences on YouTube, apparently, and comedians and comedy acts alike have benefitted from YouTube's non-traditional platform which allows for people and acts that don't fit any usual mold. One such act is Smosh, the hilarious comedy duo who has spawned a host of specials, merchandising, and even a movie. They are one of the most-followed channels on YouTube today. Bo Burnham also got his start here, posting silly videos of himself singing off-kilter songs in his bedroom. In the beginning, he made the videos to amuse his family and friends, but it wasn't long after that Netflix and others began knocking at his door. His first Netflix special, *Words Words Words*, was an unmitigated success, and he has since gone on to do more comedy specials, as well write and direct the 2018 hit movie, *Thirteen*.

The channel ||Superwoman|| has launched the career of Lilly Singh, a multitalented actress, comedian, and rapper who has one of the most popular YouTube channels out there. Singh uses her urban girl savvy along with her Indian heritage to create comedic crossover videos that humorously explore odd couplings, such as a Bollywood movie with rap music or doing a serious newscast in the guise of a popular rapper. She has been cast in Bollywood films and still maintains her explosively funny channel.

In the world of entertainment, we mustn't forget the gamers—these host some of the most successful channels in YouTube history. PewDiePie is inarguably a YouTube sensation, despite the many controversies he has set off in the last few years (approach his channel with caution, as his unorthodox views are considered offensive by many, this writer included). There is also MatPat (his screen name) who has created the very popular YouTube channels, Game Theory, and Film Theory, as well as MatPat's Game Lab on YouTube Red. His business is everything to do with gaming, from behind the scenes theory to front of the house commentary and beyond. His views reach almost two billion with over 13 million subscribers. These are just two examples among many, as gamers on YouTube have amassed a huge and dedicated following.

As you can clearly see, arts and entertainment is a huge sector within the YouTube family of channels, no doubt for good reason, as YouTube is primarily an entertainment site. What the most successful people and groups have is a unique voice and point of view with well-scripted entertainment, be it music or sketches or analytical glosses, who work hard to reach a broad audience of viewers and keep producing content in order to keep viewers watching and listening. Overnight success is a misnomer, for certain—even the acts that seem to come out of nowhere have spent many years cultivating and honing their skills and image—and it takes dedication and times to achieve this level of success. Nevertheless, these stories should encourage you to reach for the stars, almost literally!

Chapter 11: Politics and History

While everything on YouTube should, technically speaking, be entertaining, it is not the case that all of the content available is limited to the arts and entertainment industry. As the popularity of cable television exploded over the last thirty years, news shows emerged as one of the most lucrative niches—and the same goes for YouTube channels, as well. Channels that focus on the news of the day, political information, and historical context are also quite popular with many viewers. Some take on a gritty edge, such as Vice, while others use a blend of humor and satire to critique the politics of the moment. Still, others use interesting historical fact and stories to highlight particular moments, movements, ideas, and innovation.

Vice, obviously, directly targets an audience of young adventurous types—typically male, one might suggest—in its biting news stories and hard-nosed reporting styles that harken back to an age of independent journalists on the ground, out in the field. Not without controversy, Vice covers stories that lurk outside the mainstream or takes stories that are mainstream and covers them with a twist. Vice's success lies in its unique and unstintingly critical voice; its draw reaches far beyond YouTube though that is where many people go to find its content. One of the successful techniques that Vice uses to keep its information organized and to keep viewers interested is to arrange many of their stories into playlists. Unlike what you may be interested in doing on YouTube, Vice relies on numerous independent reporters to create its content—but this is a successful business model that news organizations have been utilizing for more than a century. If you have a unique take on politics, history, or news, then you might look to channels like this one to inspire your own organization.

The Young Turks is another media outlet that focuses its YouTube channel on progressive politics and other news of the day including, entertainment and popular culture. The organization has been around for quite a while, getting its start on Sirius radio and jumping to the web later. Their YouTube channel has more than four million subscribers, and each of their segments plays like a regular network television segment with five minutes to fifteen minutes (a la the segments on the long-running *60 Minutes*) in length. Again, they operate as an organization with many contributors to maintain the pace of the videos. With any channel that is dedicated to news or politics, the pace of uploading videos must be quite quick in order to capitalize on the biggest stories of the day; thus, it usually takes more than one person or one very dedicated person to manage this kind of outlet.

It should also be noted that traditional news outlets have also managed to capitalize on YouTube, with networks such as ABC, CNN, and BBC all running popular YouTube sites. These channels operate much more traditionally, which is actually part of the strength of the YouTube brand: not only does it allow traditional broadcasts to reach traditional audiences, but it also allows for upstarts, like the ones mentioned above, to have space on the platform. This kind of broad-scale freedom fosters cross-pollination of audiences, wherein someone who would likely listen to a traditional broadcast might also be drawn by the brasher Vice or the more pop culture Young Turks—and vice versa, of course. This is simply to point out that your audience base can change over time, depending on how your channel is linked up to other ones, and so on. This is why optimizing your keywords and understanding how YouTube searches work is absolutely crucial toward picking up a large audience, such as the size you'll need to be able to eventually monetize your channel.

There are also individual success stories amid the political and news niche on YouTube: Philip DeFranco started out as an individual vlogger on YouTube who created charmingly offbeat videos with a humorous take on the news and politics. Since then, his channel SourceFed has become one of the most popular YouTube channels, with a cast of quirky and funny satirists who both report and parody the politics of the day. The success of DeFranco points out what cable television learned a long time ago: blending politics and humor is one of the most successful formulas that you can dream up: think *The Daily Show*, or more recently, *Last Week Tonight with John Oliver*, or even the mainstream networks' increasing use of their late-night line-ups to critique and comment on politics in their monologues and skits (Stephen Colbert, Jimmy Kimmel, James Corden, to name a few). Comedians throughout the twentieth and twenty-first century have also capitalized on this formula. It's a winning combination if you have personality, comedic timing, good writing, and a keen sense of what's happening in the here and now.

There are also several channels that simply focus on historical context, rather than explicitly diving into daily news or current politics. Among the best of these are Alternate History Hub, which dreams up scenarios wherein it imagines what would have happened if a historical event had occurred in a slightly different way, and Simple History, which tells interesting historical stories using simple animation and clearly narrated scripts. There are also channels devoted to history that use the same kinds of mash-ups mentioned above, in combining humorous satire with historical commentary. Overly Sarcastic Productions is one of those channels, and their name says it all; this channel specializes in videos about literature, mythology, and history using sarcastic humor and funny parody. This pastiche is successful for those viewers who want something informative but also playful. Naturally, there are history channels that are devoted to particular events in history, such as Baz Battles, which, as its name suggests, focuses on famous battles (sometimes fictional, mostly historical) and battlefield tactics to illuminate the vagaries of war. Historia Civilis, with its nearly half a million subscribers, focuses solely on Rome and Roman history. If you happen to be an amateur aspect on some facet of history that hasn't yet been explored on YouTube, then this might be the niche for you.

Chapter 12:
Fitness and Advice

Among the many popular sites on YouTube, fitness has obviously captured a large slice of the audience. Indeed, fitness videos on YouTube could theoretically be attractive to any audience, or at least to audiences who have been drawn to YouTube for something else in the entertainment realm and stumble upon the treasure trove of varying workouts. The advantage of YouTube is in its flexibility, as the fitness videos you find will be of varying lengths testing varying abilities. It can easily be said that there is something for nearly everyone—if not everyone—within the YouTube platform in this category. Yoga itself has spawned an entire fitness niche of its own on YouTube. Alongside the self-improvement bent of the fitness category on YouTube exists the plethora of how-to channels, with home improvement channels being particularly popular. Last, we'll take a look at some science channels that fit somewhere in between advice and education.

One of the most subscribed fitness channels; FitnessBlender delivers exactly what its name promises. A truly word-of-mouth sensation, FitnessBlender offers not only full-length exercise routines but also individualized programs and other health advice, including nutritious recipes. The channel has uploaded over five hundred workout videos thus far, and one of the secrets to its success—and an enticing draw to get viewers to subscribe—is that it offers new workout videos at the beginning of each workweek. Thus, FitnessBlender functions to keep its audience interested in its variety and thoroughness. Another element of the success of the channel is the feeling of personal connection with the husband and wife team who run the channel; they strive to communicate with their audience and are unabashedly available to answer questions or proffer advice. This is clearly a piece of advice for the beginner: creating a personal connection to your audience is often a crucial piece of the puzzle leading to success. FitnessBlender is not the only channel to engage in this, and fitness isn't the only niche to utilize this technique; it's a bit of good advice for anyone wanting to grow an audience for their YouTube channel.

As mentioned above, within the niche of fitness itself is the ubiquitous arena of yoga videos.

Because of yoga's popularity (and its attendant fitness style, pilates) among celebrities, it has become one of the most lucrative fitness industries today. Amongst one the most popular Yoga channels is Yoga with Adrienne which offers routines from the simple to the expert, with the folksy, charming presence of Adrienne always there to remind you to do only what you find most comfortable. Her friendly encouragement, along with a variety of routines of various lengths, has made her channel one of the most subscribed fitness channels on YouTube. There is also PsycheTruth, which certainly focuses on yoga but also a forum wherein health gurus of various kinds are able to share information with each other and with the audience. Boho Beautiful is another channel which is as beautiful to look at as it is advanced in technique. This channel also features men doing yoga, which is somewhat of a rarity, at least on YouTube.

YouTube's how-to channels are so numerous and so varied that it would be impossible to put them into one easy category. Just about any hobby or amateur skill that you can dream up has a representative how-to video for others to learn about it or hone their current abilities. This category is an excellent example of the pleasures and pitfalls of YouTube: first, many of the how-to videos are either amateurish or obscure, and this might give you an indication of where you might find an audience by producing better material on a particular sub-category. Second, the field is rather saturated, so it's best you do some research before you decide to jump on this as your niche; having an original voice and clarity of purpose is fairly crucial to standing out in the crowd, so to speak. Last, these are still yet tremendously popular videos, so there is something to be said about pursuing this as a niche. It helps to have an arc, as many of these videos are relegated to one time bits of advice rather than long-running channels with a clear core message.

Many of those that are able to create a channel within this niche area related to home improvements, in particular. Under that broad category resides any number of smaller nuts-and-bolts videos to fill out your playlists and create a broad arc. Think of one the longest-running and most popular home improvement shows ever conceived, *This Old House.* In the course of one season, the show focuses on the renovation of one particular house, addressing everything from contracting and building to electrical and plumbing to landscaping and decorating along the way. Of course, *This Old House* has parlayed much of its material into a very popular YouTube channel, as well. One of the newcomers with a broad audience is House Improvements, which provides very simple and straightforward videos on any aspect of home improvement. In addition, we have seen over recent years the growth of various niche ideas within the broad arena of "home," in general—decorating, beautification, Decluttering and so on have all made inroads in YouTube popularity. More on that in the following chapter.

Last, there are a handful of excellent science channels, with a niche somewhere in between general education and advice or how-to. Indeed, some of the best science channels have more subscribers than the most popular fitness, history, or news channels. There is a thirst out there for unusual or helpful scientific information, and these channels deliver with a broad range of styles. The most successful science channels are ones that combine verifiable factual information with a quirky and entertaining style of delivery. For example, AsapSCIENCE uses animation, humorous characters, and a hefty dose of statistical and factual information to discuss scientific topics as diverse as the anti-vaxxer movement and the age-old chicken and egg question (which came first?). Another popular channel, TheBackyardScientist, employs direct experimentation to test scientific theories, a style made popular by the long-running

Discovery Channel show *Mythbusters*. The most effective science channels are marked by unique characters and quirky techniques to keep audiences tuning in—a helpful tip in a building just about any successful YouTube presence.

Chapter 13: Cooking and Home

In addition to the focus on general how-to and advice channels, YouTube also has a plethora of channels devoted to cooking, from the general basics to the specific cuisine. Over the last couple of decades—really, since the advent of the Food Network—the popularity of food, cooking, and chef-themed shows have exploded. The old Food Network stars, such as Emeril Lagasse and Mario Batali, have been superseded by a new generation of talent, beginning with stars like Guy Fieri and the late Anthony Bourdain (of the Travel Channel and CNN), and onto even fresher faces like those that crop up on YouTube. It seems that the public fascination with trying new foods, watching celebrity chefs, and honing their skills in the kitchen has not yet reached its peak. Alongside this are other channels celebrating home and hearth, from decorating and Decluttering to lifestyle and image.

One extraordinarily popular YouTube channel, Tasty, has over fifteen million subscribers and growing. Its success is based on its season-wide focus on a particular story arc, such as Season 1's focus on giant-sized food recipes or Season's 2 challenge to chefs to make real food out of conceptual drawings. So, even though it posts loads of videos, it has some cohesion to keep subscribers interested in watching through an entire season of short episodes. In addition, it organizes its content into different playlists to appeal to varying audience members. It also posts a new video every day, and while this is not a feasible goal for a beginner who is working on her own, it is certainly part of its success—consistency and new content. The variety is endless, but there is also a satisfying storyline to connect the dots between many of their videos, a tip to keep in mind for your own enterprise.

There are also channels devoted to one kind of cooking or one type of cuisine, of course. For example, How to Cook That features videos that focus on baking, in particular cookies, cakes, and chocolate dishes. MaangChi specializes in Korean cooking solely, and some have credited it with helping to expand the reach of Korean food; ten years ago it was hard to find kimchi—now its ubiquitous. There are also corporate brands out there that are using YouTube to reach a broader audience, such as the British chef and brand Jamie Oliver and the glossy magazine Bon Appetite. YouTube is a way to keep these names and brands fresh and present in consumer's minds. Taking a look at these will give you a sense of what a more traditional organization looks like in comparison to the newcomers.

In addition to cooking channels, YouTube hosts a number of channels devoted to other aspects of keeping a home and family happy. Home improvement channels were discussed in the previous chapter, but there are also numerous channels focusing on home décor, from high-end interior design to DIY-type decorative projects. House and Home are one the more popular channels, offering videos of whole home tours so you can see how an interior design project goes from one end of the house to the other, from the greatest to the smallest detail. There is also Three Birds Renovations which shows the potential of the lucrative house flipping business with spectacular design in mind. As with the home improvement shows, the most successful channels will have a series of episodes with an overarching theme involved. For someone wanting to start a channel on making over a house, be aware that you have much competition, but that there is still much demand. Choose a big, interesting and unique project that you can follow through with a series of videos. With a strong script and an engaging personality, this kind of channel can work with diligent focus.

Of course, the reach of Marie Kondo goes far beyond her YouTube channel. With several books under her belt and a well-respected Netflix series, Kondo isn't just a YouTube star. Yet, the appeal of her brand—and her channel—are well-suited to the aesthetic of YouTube, with short and accessible videos combined with a unique idea and a winning personality. It's also notable in that Kondo has been extraordinarily successful at cross-pollinating her brand: clips from her Netflix show appear on her YouTube channel, and naturally, she is spread across social media in general. The Kondo craze is a prime example of how promoting your passion project across various media outlets is one of the surest ways to find unexpectedly significant success.

Last, there are a set of channels that are devoted to various oddities that are marginally relevant to this section on a home (truly, they aren't quite categorizable). For example, shopping spree (or "haul") videos are quite popular among a certain segment of the (largely female-driven) audience. I would loosely call these videos lifestyle videos, a kind of wish fulfillment for attaining the trendiest merchandise from the most elite sources. These videos are a clear opportunity for established brands to make use of YouTube influencers and drum up sales, but they are also enjoyable in their own right to some people. These are aspirational videos, for the most part, wherein we aspire to look and feel a certain way by emulating the lifestyle of someone marginally (or fabulously) famous. Zoella is a popular channel with over eleven million subscribers; the channel is a loosely organized set of videos that serve as the new wave of 21st-century advertising.

The other odd duck in the YouTube age is the exploding popularity of unboxing videos: there is a loose affiliation with the above in terms of aspirational intention, but the reason that many people seem to enjoy unboxing videos is simply to relive the element of emotion that goes along with finding out what's in the box—a sort of daily reenactment of our childlike excitement at the holidays. Again, these videos tie in with brand marketing and the newly emerging role of internet influencer. Unbox Therapy currently has more than fourteen million followers who watch host Lew Later unbox the latest technology gadgets. Who knows? Find a niche within that specialized niche and unbox something new.

Chapter 14: Travel and Adventure

From home and hearth to exploring the world, travel and adventure channels also get a lot of YouTube play. It's not difficult to understand the appeal: gorgeous videos of faraway locations and/or spectacular stunts (usually in faraway locations) capture the imagination of a wide audience. These channels go beyond the typical family vacation vlog or personal growth video into the exotic and the exciting. Making these videos is surely the province of a particular kind of personality, but making your mark in these arenas need not require you travel the world or dive off cliffs. An engaging personality with an intriguing story and some stunning video can break into this category with persistence and energy.

Most of the popular travel channels on YouTube engage in a particular niche within the category. For example, Mark Wiens, with his more than four million subscribers, focuses on travel for the sake of foodie adventures—and, for watchers, foodie voyeurism. His world travels may not be accessible to everyone, but watching him wax poetic about particular foods in particular locales calls to mind some of the best food broadcasts in the last decade (Anthony Bourdain and Andrew Zimmern chief among those). Collin Abroadcast stars a very different kind of personality who, in addition to the clever name, spends time trying to cleverly expose counterfeits in addition to engaging in exploits abroad to try to stay abroad (that is, make money). There is also the simple if aptly, named the channel, Stories, which showcases little known stories from unique peoples and cultures around the world. Decidedly more highbrow than the previous two examples, Stories is a channel for viewers with wide-ranging interests and curiosity. Like many successful YouTube channels, Stories is a pastiche, in this case of on-the-ground reporting, creative dreaming, and a commitment to social justice. In terms of what's available currently on YouTube, many of the most popular travel channels focus on food; there is still room for travel channels with a different primary agenda in mind.

The adventure-type channel is an entire niche in and of itself on the YouTube platform. It is almost always associated with travel—usually difficult and exotic travel, as the category would suggest—and with some sort of extreme sport. One of the most inspirational of these channels is Fearless and Far, created by Mike Corey. With a quarter of a million subscribers, Corey travels the globe in order to face his fears, while also engaging with locals in a fun, respectful, and empathetic way. His channel takes the viewer to lesser-known, exotic locales, helping him to stand apart from the crowd. Other well-known videographers on the adventure circuit are Matthew Karsten and Adrienne Parzel. There are numerous adventure travelers out there with amazing videos from which to choose. For the beginning YouTuber, these kinds of channels are almost certainly out of reach; however, you can learn much from watching the personalities, the filming techniques, and the storylines about what makes a successful foray into a travel channel, in general.

The reach of these influencers is beyond the scope of a newcomer to YouTube. But there is a dearth of channels that cover a kind of middle ground, between the amateur vacation vlog channel to the professional travel-adventurer. As with many channels that have been discussed throughout this book, one of the more successful ways to gain ground on YouTube is to invent a new category within a category by combining popular elements from different niches, such as humor with politics or travel with social justice. Your unique voice need not emanate from a far-off location of from the top of a jagged mountain; rather, it might come from redefining what we think of as travel. Take a year-long tour of your home town, for example, and create a story arc that takes on importance and meaning over time. What does it mean to live in "real" America? Or, how does one define travel within a region of dwindling resources? Depending on where you are and what your interests are, you could easily redefine the category of travel channel. Another potential idea is to take a passion or hobby of yours and turn it into a kind of travel adventure, seeking out the best or weirdest or both on your self-defined adventures. This is the beauty of YouTube: the limits of content are barred only (or almost only) by the limits of your imagination. After reviewing several dozen channels, you might discover that your exact interest is something that doesn't quite exist yet there is enough overlap with other niches to get a foothold. Think big, plan well, and execute professionally, and you might just have a new hit on your hands.

Chapter 15:
General Educational

Finally, while YouTube is primarily about entertainment, it is also true that many—if not most—people enjoy a little educational content with their entertainment or vice versa. Indeed, some of the most successful YouTube channels are an amalgam of information and enjoyment. Certainly, the best educational channels out there encourage its target audience to learn while having fun, and there are some who argue that YouTube and other platforms like it are re-envisioning what 21st-century education looks like—or should look like. New kinds of knowledge and skills are needed for a new era, and YouTube offers a microcosm of how a re-thinking of curriculum might eventually occur. Aside from this, many educational channels on YouTube are a pastiche of how-to, exploration, and general discovery of interesting information. Regardless of intention, these generalized channels—with thought-out scripts and good editing—reach a very broad audience in many cases.

For an example of a fun romp, The King of

Random has over ten million subscribers and a surprising variety of video. One of the keys to the channel's success is that its look is very consistent and its content organized, even though the content of the videos themselves range widely. This is noteworthy in suggesting that any channel should contain some cohesive elements to pull it together, whether it be episodic, like filming a television series, or stylistic, like creating a particular image that is instantly recognizable.

On the other end of the spectrum are the educational and corporate giants such as National Geographic, an age-old brand that is trying, as many traditional companies are, to engage a new generation of viewers on this new platform. For the beginning YouTuber, NatGeo's channel is a place to explore in order to formulate new ideas and to think about particular niches upon which you could capitalize. Because it is in a fairly traditional episodic format, the channel's playlists can give you an idea of how to organize a particular set of episodes in a particular way—chronologically, categorically, geographically, or otherwise—which helps for cohesive viewing. For a less but still traditional channel, Ted-Ed's educational channel is in collaboration with the ever-popular TED Talks and its various offshoots. Ted-Ed aims to provide other educators with tools and presentations about topics and issues;

this channel is essentially a resource for other educators, providing content for free and fair use. It also employs graphics and animation in ways that make the presentations seem more contemporary and fun. This is an excellent channel to review if you have intentions of breaking into the educational niche; it shows how one single topic can generate several short, easily digestible videos making for learning that feels easy and enjoyable.

CrashCourse is another example of an educational channel that takes up a wide variety of material with the help of numerous experts in their field. The cohesiveness of the channel, like The King of Random's channel, comes out of the consistent aesthetic—a trait that cannot be emphasized enough in creating a channel that grabs and keeps viewers. Its aim is fairly traditional—teaching familiar subjects in everything from physics to literature to the US government—in updated and animated ways. The, even more, well-known Khan Academy is another model of this type, with a twist. One of the most phenomenal stories of the power of YouTube, Khan Academy was (almost accidentally) created by Salman Khan to help a young relative struggling with math get his lessons down. Because they were living geographically apart, Khan came up with engaging and interactive videos to walk him through particular math lessons. From this humble start, the Khan Academy has grown into an enormous, multi-national, non-profit entity dedicated to providing quality education free of charge to students across the world. His methods have been replicated in classrooms around the world, and his Academy has inspired new ways of teaching and of learning. Again, these examples reveal how a new approach to education, in general, is clearly emerging.

Alltime 10s is an amalgamation channel that brings together various other YouTube videos in order to compile a list of the "top ten"—an organizing impulse that most of us utilize or respond to on a daily basis. Because its content pool is so vast, the information doesn't really have a clear coherence; rather, it's the overall concept of compiling a top ten list that is the hook. This is another example of how a simple idea properly executed can generate great success.

Channels that fit into the general education category are numerous and are, to varying degrees, actually educational. If you have ever had an interest in teaching or training, these are a few of the many examples upon which you might mold your own channel. These channels are different from the how-to channels in that they are not emphasizing a skill to be practiced and perfected—an admirable goal in and of itself—but rather a way of analytical thinking grounded in recognized fields. As colleges who defend general education emphasizes, critical thinking skills are just as crucial as specialized knowledge for any professional or citizen of the world. You, too, can make your mark if you want to create a unique educational niche.

Conclusion

Starting a YouTube channel is a fun, exciting—and potentially lucrative—way in which to showcase your creative talents. YouTube purports to have something for everything, and you could easily be a part of that plethora of entertainment, knowledge, and advice that resides on the site. As the format for most content keeps changing rapidly, streaming is fast becoming the primary method by which most people get their entertainment and information. There are multiple opportunities for someone who has good ideas and a unique vision to jump into this arena—having fun and making money to boot.

Now that you have learned how to start a YouTube channel and maximize its potential, you understand the many reasons why putting in the time and effort to create a YouTube channel is an excellent idea, from promoting a business that you already have to monetizing your favorite hobby or skill. You have learned, step by step, how to set up and run a successful YouTube channel, as well as gleaned some ideas of what might be possible if your channel becomes a hit—there are opportunities beyond YouTube to be gained, as well. The numerous success stories already in play on YouTube that you have read about, from educational channels to cooking and home-style shows to politics and entertainment channels, should inspire you to do more. There is literally content for everyone out there; you merely have to develop and promote your niche.

So, now that you are inspired and motivated—and well-versed in the practical components of how to begin and grow your channel—get started on creating your successful YouTube channel today! It only takes a bit of time, an interesting idea, and a modicum of determination to become the next YouTube sensation.

www.ingramcontent.com/pod-product-compliance
Lightning Source LLC
Chambersburg PA
CBHW070423220526
45466CB00004B/1525